# CONTENTS

# INTRODUCTION

Andrew fitted the key in the front door and turned it. He pushed the door open, and they stepped inside. Everything was exactly the same as it was two days before, except for one huge difference: the baby that Hilary was carrying in her arms.

They suspected then, and proved over the next few months, that that little person represented the biggest change that had ever happened in their lives—bigger even than getting married. Suddenly things that were once all-important (job, vacations, dining out) seemed to shrink, and things they'd never thought much about (health, diet, lifestyle) began to assume a new importance.

And over everything was this thought, *We want the best for our child.*

Of course they did. Everyone does.

From the moment you know a baby is on the way, and perhaps even before that, you will do everything possible to ensure that he or she is born fit, well, and happy.

And there's so much advice, from mother and mother-in-law and all your friends who are parents. Suddenly everyone seems an instant expert on the subject! People want to lend you articles and magazines, and, of course, there's also the professional advice of the staff at the physician's office.

By the time you've listened and read and watched everything, you may well feel totally confused. It's strange how such a completely natural thing as having a baby can suddenly become so complicated.

So let's try to uncomplicate it!

For your baby to grow up into a truly healthy, well-balanced adult, each part of its being needs to be nurtured. From the moment of birth he will need to be helped to develop physically, intellectually, emotionally, and spiritually.

That is to say, you want the child to have a healthy body, a lively and inquiring mind, to experience love and bonding, and to become a happy, whole, and "good" person. If you neglect one of these elements at the

# WHAT DOES MY CHILD REALLY NEED?

*How to Give Your Child the Best Start in Life*

CHRISTINE AND DAVID WINTER

BARBOUR
PUBLISHING, INC.
Uhrichsville, Ohio

Text © 1999 by David and Christine Winter. Original edition published in English under the title *The Best for Your Child* by Lion Publishing plc, Oxford, England. Copyright © Lion Publishing plc 1999.

This edition © 2001 by Barbour Publishing, Inc.

ISBN 1-58660-273-X

All Scripture quotations are taken from the HOLY BIBLE, NEW INTERNATIONAL VERSION®. NIV®. Copyright © 1973, 1978, 1984 by International Bible Society. Used by permission of Zondervan Publishing House. All rights reserved.

Published by Barbour Publishing, Inc., P. O. Box 719, Uhrichsville, Ohio 44683 http://www.barbourbooks.com

 Member of the
Evangelical Christian
Publishers Association

Printed in the United States of America.

expense of another, you may deprive your child of a vital part of what it means to be truly human.

This little book is mostly concerned with the fourth element: spiritual development, what we call the "fourth dimension" of child development. We feel that it's in danger of being missed in the flood of advice and guidance which new parents are given.

When a new baby arrives, many young parents feel that it's a kind of miracle, a gift from God. Well, God has not only given you this wonderful gift, He wants to give your child good things, too.

Christians call God "Father," and that is significant (Romans 8:15). For, like a good parent, God not only wants the best for the world and the best for us; God also wants, every bit as much as you do, the best for your child.

# GOOD BABY!

*A well-meaning friend peers into the crib, makes all the right admiring noises and then asks, "Is she a good baby?"*

What she meant was, "Does your baby sleep through the night, feed at regular intervals, and when awake smile and gurgle rather than cry?" Those questions reflect how we feel, how pleasant or stressful an experience we find caring for a baby is. They aren't questions of morality.

A baby that cries is not being "bad," and a baby that smiles and gurgles is not being "good." It's actually unhelpful to label infant behavior in that way.

Small babies respond positively to things like food, comfort, warmth, human company, and love. Given these things, they may be regarded as "good" babies.

But plenty of babies don't respond like this. No matter what you do, the baby simply goes on crying. Food, comfort, warmth, human company, and all the love you can summon up seem to make no difference! Every time you put the baby down to sleep, she starts to cry. Sometimes she is inconsolable even when you hold her in your arms. In those circumstances it may be quite hard to tell yourself that your baby isn't being "bad."

Evenings are often bad times for parents and small babies, because parents are tired, exhausted even. The baby may subconsciously pick up these vibes of tiredness and tension. Or the baby may simply have colic or be hungry. Perhaps she doesn't need sleep and just wants your company. At the very time of the day when you feel most under pressure, this extra demand comes—and it can sometimes be the last straw!

The trouble with calling this sort of behavior by small babies "good" or "bad" is that you begin to think that it must somehow be your fault.

If your baby is "bad," then surely you must be a bad parent? There must be something you've done that you shouldn't have done. . .or something you've not done that you should be doing. And then you start feeling guilty.

Or you decide that this particular child is "troublesome," "awkward," or "difficult." That may shape your attitude and feelings toward her for the rest of her life. . . "She always was the difficult one!"

But a new baby is only aware of feelings. She doesn't work things out logically. She recognizes feelings of hunger, discomfort, pain, and loneliness; and crying is simply a way of asking that these feelings be dealt with. That is how a baby survives. And it's certainly not a matter of being "good" or "bad."

# SHAPING BEHAVIOR

Where baby's behavior is concerned, the best advice is to go with his or her needs. If the baby is hungry, offer a feeding. If the baby cries, offer a cuddle. Babies that are wide awake aren't going to be tricked into falling asleep, so talking to them, or putting them where they can watch you, is a better idea than optimistically consigning them to their cribs.

"But I don't want to spoil her!" parents often say. They fear that if they give in to baby's crying they will be making "a rod for their own backs," and there will be people who will warn you of that danger.

But responding to a baby's needs isn't to "spoil" him. In the early months of the baby's life, he is simply learning to feel safe with you; learning to be loved, if you like, as you cuddle him, talk to him, feed, and comfort him.

Baby trusts you. And that trust is the

single most important element in the relationship between a parent and a child.

But a baby quickly learns one simple, basic rule: If you cry, you get attention. And in common with every other human being, Baby likes having attention. This isn't bad in itself, but as he grows, a child has to learn to fit in with the rest of the family's needs.

**When Baby cries.** It's easy to imagine the scene. Mother or father settles baby down to sleep. Baby starts crying, obviously wanting to be with them. But they know that Baby is tired and needs to sleep.

So. . .leave her there—or pick her up? It's the oldest dilemma facing a parent.

Several courses of action are possible.

The baby can be left to cry, while the parents tell themselves that they will pick her up if she's still crying in a few minutes' time.

Or distractions can be provided: a mobile, a teddy, music, or rocking the cradle. And very probably one of these will do the trick, and the little eyes will eventually close and the crying turn to mumbling and the mumbling to blissful silence.

Or, of course, the parent can pick up the baby and probably stop the crying on the spot. But to pick her up reinforces the idea that crying gains attention.

The baby cried. . .and the baby got attention. The message is unmistakable.

**The need for consistency.** Of course, there is crying and crying. The crying of pain or hunger needs attention. The crying that simply means "I don't want to go to sleep" is in a quite different category. Most parents quickly learn to distinguish between the two.

As the baby reaches six months or so, routine becomes more important. About now, those four or five feedings a day change into three meals plus a morning or evening feeding. Baby will be awake more during the day, and many (but not all) will now be sleeping right through the night.

So a routine becomes established—and it's quite a relief! But then, just when it seems nicely in place, the baby changes his habits.

The cause may be things like teething or a minor illness or infection. But getting the child back into a routine is not easy. To do so may require perseverance. It will definitely require consistency. If you decide you are not going to pick the child up every time he cries, in order to reestablish a helpful routine, then it's important to stick by that. The alternative is that the child learns that by crying he can make you change your mind. The result will not be less crying but more!

By the end of the first year, children have quite a highly developed sense of their own selves. They know what they want and begin to develop strategies for "getting their own way." Crying is not by any means the only strategy. Refusing food can be just as upsetting to the parents as crying.

But the dominant motive for a child's behavior at this age is simply curiosity.

A younger baby will put a toy in his mouth.

The six to nine month old will hold it, turn it over, look at it—and then probably try throwing it.

When the child starts crawling, nothing is safe! Mother needs nine sets of eyes, including one in the back of her head. Junior can't be left unattended even for a few seconds.

Suddenly your "baby" is consumed by an insatiable curiosity about everything—but has absolutely no sense of danger.

The only answer for a parent is consistency. When you make rules for your baby's safety, try to stick to them.

If a child approaches a "no-no" area, then it's not enough just to say "No." Remove the child from the area, at the same time saying "No." And do it as often as it takes.

Patience, consistency, and alertness are your best allies at this age.

# "I WANT!"

*It's a wonderful sight to see a mother and baby "talking" to each other. Mother uses words—though some may be a bit peculiar—and the baby smiles and gurgles back. Real communication is taking place, and both are very satisfied.*

Soon, recognizable sounds replace the gurgles: "Da-da" and "Ma-ma," to be followed by proper words like "cat," "car," "hello," "ball," and so on. It was surprising to hear of one child's first recognizable words. Pushing her brother out of the way, she uttered a whole sentence: "I want Mommy!"

Now, was that "good" or "bad"? It was good that she had not only begun to speak but had been able to express so clearly what she wanted. It was natural that her very first request was self-centered. After all, she wasn't yet old enough to realize that her brother might also want Mommy.

A small child's experience of the world is obviously very limited. It's a world in which he or she is at the center.

That, after all, is the experience of babyhood. Everything focuses on the baby's needs, the baby's welfare, the baby's routine. It's not surprising if they get the idea that their wants are the most important things in the world. And it's also not surprising that the first sentence they put together is often "I want."

"I want! I want" is probably going to be the most common phrase in a child's vocabulary over the first few years of life. It can have a wide variety of meanings, from a simple desire for the fulfillment of basic needs to a more complicated desire for pleasure for her own sake.

So the child says "I want Mommy" when she needs security, "I want dinner" when she's hungry, and "I want to play with your handbag" or "I want to touch the VCR" when she wants to satisfy her curiosity or try out a new experience.

There will be times when the "I want"

demands what the parent is not at the moment able or willing to provide. "I want more chocolate," "I want potato chips," or even "I don't want to go to bed" may provoke a collision of wills!

These two different kinds of "wanting" need to be distinguished.

The first sort—for the fulfilling of basic needs—has to be met in order to let the child grow up in a healthy and balanced way. A child needs love, security, food, and acceptance. She also needs to be able to develop skills and satisfy her curiosity.

But the second kind of "wanting" also expresses the basic self-centeredness of human beings: "I like it so I want it, and I'm going to have it."

Children learn by watching what you do.

That makes it very important that parents should not just *tell* their children that they can't have everything they want, but *show* them, by their own example, that they accept the principle themselves. It's not much use telling a child that she can't have what she wants if she can see that her parents always seem to have exactly what *they* want!

**Giving what is best.** What children have to learn is that although they are loved, they can't always be the center of attention and have everything they want.

The parents also have something to learn: that loving their children doesn't mean always giving them what they want, but it does mean giving them what is best. It's the way God deals with us, whom He calls His "children" (John 1:12). He doesn't give us what we want but what is best for us.

So the basic principle in responding to a child's "I want" is to ensure that, as far as you are able, he has those things which he needs, and sometimes can also have the things which he wants, but that he shouldn't constantly have what he wants on demand.

Later, as he gets older, he will come to learn that his wants (and even his needs) have to be balanced against other people's.

Today the potential for choice for the toddler is enormous.

Fish sticks or cheeseburger?

Blue pants or red ones?

White socks with stripes or the little yellow ones with bears?

Will he choose to play with the bricks, or watch a video, or even play a computer game?

A range of choice like this can be totally overwhelming for a two or three year old.

For the very small child, offering endless choices is just confusing.

Choices such as when we go to bed, what to have for dinner, and whether to go for a walk probably should always be parental decisions at this stage. Junior can then be left to decide such things as whether Mommy or Daddy puts him to bed.

# RIGHT AND WRONG

*Most parents would agree that part of their responsibility to their children is to teach them the difference between right and wrong and then to help them to choose right rather than wrong.*

It's an important task and a difficult one.
When do you start?

How do you do it?

What are the limits?

When is a baby old enough to be able to understand the difference between "right" and "wrong" behavior?

Children in their very early years are more receptive to ideas and more open to "conditioning" than at any other stage of life. What we learn when we are very tiny we never forget. That can be quite a worrying thought for parents!

How do you know what is right? In the Bible, Jesus sums up what is "right" in these words:

" 'Love the Lord your God with all your heart and with all your soul and with all your strength and with all your mind'; and, 'Love your neighbor as yourself' " (Luke 10:27).

To take the second of these principles first, "loving your neighbor as yourself" surely means that you should respect and treat other people as you would like to be treated; in fact, to value them as much as you value yourself.

Can a small child be taught that principle?

Children learn first of all by example. They learn about loving and respecting other people from the way they themselves are treated.

As babies they learned to smile and coo because someone smiled and cooed at them. They learned to make sounds and talk because someone talked to them. And as they get older they learn to share things with other people because other people share with them.

In all of this kind of learning their parents are the most influential teachers. The child learns not just from how he or she is treated by the parents but also from how the parents treat each other.

If the parents don't respect each other, it is going to be hard for the child to learn respect. If parents shout and are abusive, in no time at all the child will be copying that behavior.

But children can create their own conflicts, too.

Two toddlers want to play with the same toy. Both grab it, and neither of them will let go. Usually the older or stronger one will eventually snatch it away and even, perhaps, hit or bite the other child. If they are more evenly matched, a fight ensues.

How do you teach your toddler what is "right" in a situation like this?

There are four steps that you can take:

You show your disapproval; you say that this behavior is "bad."

You remove the children from the situation and temporarily confiscate the toy.

You show them a better way to handle the

situation, for example, by taking turns with the toy and even learning to say "sorry" for having hit or bitten the other child.

You reassure the child that although you don't approve of her behavior on this occasion, you do still love her and forgive her.

**Setting limits**. Another way of helping children to tell right from wrong is setting the limits—or "ground rules"—for behavior at home. Sooner or later we all have to learn that throughout life we operate within limits of some kind, whether we are in school, at work, or in relation to the wider society we live in.

To a large extent these ground rules are for the child's own good. You need to explain that as often as necessary. . .and the process starts from very early days.

You warn them not to touch fire because it burns, not to play with Daddy's tools because they can hurt, not to go near the road because traffic is dangerous.

These rules aren't just nasty restrictions

thought up by grown-ups to spoil the simple pleasures of life. And neither are the "rules" God gives us for life, rules designed to help us to live happy and wholesome lives in the world He has created.

There's nothing wrong with rules as long as the one imposing them loves us and wants the best for us. That's the principle behind the limits you set for your child's behavior.

Of course, it's not only physical danger that leads us to set limits to a child's behavior. Other rules are concerned with respecting other people's rights, such as not taking property without permission, not being rude, and not saying unkind things. And some of them just have to do with the family being able to live together in peace and harmony: eating together, going on outings together, sharing things, and being loyal and supportive of each other.

It's here that the wider issues of right and wrong begin to emerge.

**Learning to be "good."** Basically, there are

two ways of helping children to be "good." One is the way of fear and the other is the way of love.

In the kind of school many older people remember, there was often a teacher who frightened you into acceptable behavior with threats of what would happen if you misbehaved. But there was also the teacher whose lessons were a joy because there was mutual trust and respect between the teacher and the class.

The first kind of teacher built up resentment and rebellion rather than a genuine love of doing what is right. The second developed trust and a sense of well-being, in which you wanted to do what was right.

Probably most parents who are seriously trying to help their children to learn right from wrong, and choose right rather than wrong, will accept that a mixture of the two approaches is appropriate.

But you need to get the balance right: no more than ten percent of threats, and at least ninety percent of love!

# INNOCENCE AND TRUST

*There are two qualities of small children which are especially attractive. They are innocent, and they are trusting.*

And, perhaps because we live in a world where innocence is quickly lost, and we all too soon learn not to be so trusting, we cherish and admire the innocence and trust of children.

The small child is an innocent abroad—a bit like Adam and Eve before they ate the fruit (Genesis 2:25)! And the toddler has an uncomplicated trust in his parents in sharp contrast with the suspicion of the adult world.

We've already seen how trust is built through the closeness of the parent/child relationship.

Through the trustworthiness of his parents the child learns to trust other people. So, how is that trust built up?

Toddlers, as we know, watch their parents' reactions to situations, and they take their cue from what they see. Take the inevitable visit to the dentist. If Mom or Dad goes cheerfully and positively into the dentist's office, the child will learn that it is not an experience to dread. But if they show anxiety, that will communicate to the child, too: Don't go to the dentist; it hurts!

The child needs to learn, of course, that not everything that happens in life will be pleasant. Inevitably, a child will experience pain sooner or later, perhaps from an illness or accident.

Scrapes, bumps, and bruises hurt, but in those moments of tears and distress they learn again that they can trust their parents to comfort them and assure them that all is well despite the pain.

**Childlike trust**. Childlike trust puts a responsibility on parents. If it is to be maintained, they must not let the child down but use that trust to build up in the child's life an appreciation of what is good and a distaste for what is bad.

You nurture trust in children by always being truthful with them. It doesn't help to say "It won't hurt" when you know it will, or "I'll be back in a minute" when you know you've got to leave your child in someone else's care for half a day. Children remember when their trust is betrayed, and the next time they may not be so trusting.

It's much better to explain that you have to go but that you're leaving something of your own with your child so that they know you're going to come back and also have something of you with them while you're away.

You evade the truth in order to spare your children pain, but in fact your strategy can rebound and cause them greater grief if they feel that you've let them down or not kept your word.

Sadly, there's also a negative aspect to the trusting nature of an innocent child. It makes them vulnerable to people whose motives are evil and who wish to cause them harm.

A trusting toddler will go off with an

unknown adult simply because he or she has learned from you to trust adults: parents, grandparents, or friends. So it is a sad fact of the world we live in that you also have to teach your children from a very early age that not all adults can be trusted. They have to be able to say "No" to the suggestions of strangers that they should go off with them.

We've said that the innocence of a child is rather like Adam and Eve before they ate the fruit in the Garden of Eden. But, like Adam and Eve, temptation and lost innocence inevitably lie ahead.

In every human being there is a capacity both for great good and great evil, and that is true even in the loveliest child.

But you can do a lot to protect that fragile innocence from outside influences by ensuring as far as you can that what comes into the home of small children will not harm them. Obviously that applies to what they may see on television, but it also applies to things you talk about in their presence and the pictures and video games and so on that are around the home, possibly in the hands of older brothers and sisters.

You can't protect children forever from all that is ugly and bad, but you can minimize its impact and delay its arrival until you can help them to deal with it at a more appropriate age.

# THE FOURTH DIMENSION

*So far we've been thinking about helping children to grow into healthy and well-adjusted adults. That means being healthy in body, mind, and emotions, and we've seen how the way children are handled from the time of their birth can help them toward that goal. But is that enough?*

As we've already suggested, there is a "fourth dimension" to a person. This is often called the "spiritual" or "moral" side of their nature.

Already we've talked about how you can help your children to distinguish between right and wrong, and protect them from bad influences on their lives while they are very young. But that's only a part of what we call "spiritual development."

"Spiritual" is an interesting word. It means "to do with our spirit": that part of us which responds to beauty, love, and inner truth. . .and to God.

"God is spirit," said Jesus (John 4:24). And this inner self—our spirit—is never completely satisfied apart from Him.

So, to be a complete person, healthy in body, mind, and spirit, our inner self needs to be in touch with God and living in harmony with Him. And that's as true of children as it is of adults.

Can anyone who has heard a child's prayers doubt for one moment that they can be "in touch" with their heavenly Father? When we were thinking about what is right and what is wrong we quoted Jesus:

> " 'Love the Lord your God with all your heart and with all your soul and with all your strength and with all your mind'; and, 'Love your neighbor as yourself' " (Luke 10:27).

At that point we talked about how a child should react to his "neighbors." But now let's ask, *How should a child relate to God?* That's the "fourth dimension" of child development, introducing them to their heavenly Father. We shall look at that in more detail in the next section.

# GOD OUR FATHER

*Christians, following Jesus, speak of God as "father." In fact, the word Jesus used really means "daddy"; it's the child's word rather than the formal, adult one. God is the ideal father— we could say, the sort of father every child should have, but sadly some don't: a father who wants the best for his children and wants his children to love him in response to his love for them.*

God showed His love by sending His Son, Jesus, into the world. More than that, He was prepared for Jesus to go all the way to death on the cross to demonstrate the extent of His love for us. Then He raised Jesus from death to life, promising that those who believe in Him will have eternal life (John 3:16–17).

We aren't suggesting that small children should be expected to understand all of that! But it's important that adults should understand the extent of God's love for us, because that's what lies behind our own relationship with God and His approach to us, and it's the basis on which we can build a child's trust in God as a heavenly Father.

Many parents would like their children to grow up to have a good moral and spiritual basis to their lives—even parents who may not be very "religious" themselves. But sometimes they wonder if it is possible, or right, to expect very young children to have a faith or belief in God.

**Can children have faith?** This must depend very largely on what parents themselves believe. Parents who have a strong religious faith will naturally want their children to grow up in that faith, whether it's Jewish, Hindu, Muslim, or Christianity.

But many parents aren't sure about what they believe. Perhaps they have a basic belief in God. Perhaps they would call themselves Christians but aren't quite sure what that involves. Not surprisingly, such parents tend to say something like, "I'm not sure, so I'll wait until the children are older and then they can decide for themselves."

It sounds very reasonable.

Others are quite clear that they'd like their children to grow up with Christian beliefs or standards but aren't sure how to go about it.

It may sound reasonable to allow your children to "make up their own minds," but you don't apply that to other things which you regard as important.

You don't let them:

- choose their own diet
- go to bed when they choose
- decide for themselves when and where they'll start their schooling.

You would say that in those areas they need your guidance—and you'd be right.

If a child's spiritual development is as important as its social, educational, or physical development, surely your "guidance" is needed here, too.

There will be plenty of opportunity for them later, when they are a good deal older, to decide whether they wish to make this faith their own.

But if you have decided that you should raise your children in the Christian faith, then there are two factors you need to bear in mind:

- First of all, they need to know about the faith.
- Then, in some way, they need to experience it.

**Where do you start?** As soon as your children are old enough to listen to stories at all, you can begin to tell simple stories about Jesus. There are plenty of lovely, colorful Bible storybooks in stores which anyone can use, suitable for all age groups, from the tiniest children through primary school age.

Babies and toddlers also love music and rhythm. They will soon become familiar with songs about God and Jesus, many of which are fun to perform with actions. Many churches have preschool groups and services where children can learn these songs and enjoy doing them with other children.

What is the object of this early teaching about God and Jesus?

It's like what we would do, if, for some reason, a child's father was going to be away from home for a long while. Mom would talk about Daddy, show the child pictures of Daddy, tell stories of Daddy, so that when he eventually came home the child would recognize this strange man as her father.

You can't see God, but you can show your children the evidence of His love and care. You can talk about Him, tell the stories of what He has done and especially about Jesus. And you can encourage them to talk to Him in simple, trusting prayer, thanking Him for the details of each day and involving Him in the little—and big—events of their lives.

In that way, God isn't remote and odd, but someone who loves them and wants to share everything in their lives with them.

Prayer with children can be marvelously simple.

"Thank You, God" is a beautiful prayer. So is "Please help me today."

Children can understand that God is part of the nice things that happen: birthdays, parties, Christmas, summer vacations. They can also understand that He can help them in the difficult and sad things: Grandpa dying or being in a hospital themselves.

Faith is believing that God hears and answers our prayers. It's believing that God loves me and wants me to love Him in response; as Jesus said, "with all your heart" (Matthew 22:37, Mark 12:30, Luke 10:27). And it's also about learning to please Him by choosing to do what is right (1 John 5:3).

# LESS THAN PERFECT

*Often parents wonder whether the way they show love to their children is the "right" way. Are they being too soft? Or too harsh? When the children misbehave and need to be punished, will they think you don't love them anymore? And how soon after that punishment should you give them a cuddle and say it's all right? Or would doing that tell the child that misbehaving doesn't really matter?*

I f we're looking for a good model of how to show love and yet guide a child away from what's bad and toward what's good, then we can't do better than see how God does it. After all, He has misbehaving children, too! Yet the Bible tells us that He loves us and values us despite that (Romans 5:8).

There's a wonderful story Jesus told of a father and a son.

The boy, in a willful gesture of defiance, takes his share of the family money and goes off to a distant city, where he squanders it all in riotous living.

He's been a real disappointment to his father. He's let him down, disgraced the family, and acted selfishly and foolishly.

Eventually, when he's run out of money and is in desperate straits, he decides to go back to his father. He's not sure how he'll be received, but, as he argues to himself, even his father's servants are better off than he is now. So he sets off for home.

And, Jesus said, "While he was still a long way off, his father saw him and was filled with compassion for him; he ran to his son, threw his arms around him and kissed him" (Luke 15:20).

Although he had disappointed his father, been foolish and willful and unkind, his father still loved him.

He learned then that love doesn't depend on the one who is loved but the one who does the loving.

God doesn't love us because we're lovely, but because, as the Bible says, "God is love" (1 John 4:8). He accepts us when we turn to Him, whatever we have done.

**Accepting children as they are**. That is really the best model of how you love your children. You don't approve of what they do wrong. You know that sometimes they will annoy and disappoint you. But you love them and accept them as they are.

Secretly you may want them to be brain surgeons or airline pilots, while they seem more interested in dodging homework and spending time out with friends or on the sports field. But you do not let your disappointment destroy your love for them.

Whatever mess they may make of their lives (to take the extreme example), you will still go on loving, accepting, and forgiving them, because that is what it means to be a parent. You will always be there to help them make that new start when, like the son in Jesus' story, they come to their senses.

And that sort of consistent, accepting love begins in the cradle.

We live in a world where people expect everything to be perfect, flawless. We would like to live in a perfect house, with a perfect garden, to dress perfectly, and look perfect ourselves. And the commercials tell us that it's possible!

But they're lying.

Life can't be perfect for everyone, everywhere, and we're deceiving ourselves if we think that it can. But we do find it hard to accept imperfection.

We must all face the fact that even today many babies are born with a handicap, sometimes slight, sometimes severe. But these children, too, have much to give and are equally deserving of a parent's love.

Wanting the best for such children certainly involves accepting and loving them and helping them to develop their full potential, even if that is less than average or less than we had hoped.

In any case, there is no such thing as a perfect child—or a perfect adult, either. There are flaws and faults in all of us, as most of us are only too aware. God accepts us as we are, without waiting for us to become perfect first. And that's a good example for parents, too.

In fact, whatever kind of child you have, wanting the best for him starts with accepting and loving the child as a person made in God's image (Genesis 1:27), of infinite value and worth (Matthew 10:29–31). Children are a precious gift of God, to be loved and cherished (Matthew 19:14).

You want to see your child develop in the best possible way, in body, mind, and spirit. . . and your love, support, example, and prayers are the means by which you help to bring it about.

# WHERE DO YOU GO FROM HERE?

*If you want to help your child to develop that "fourth dimension," and grow up as strong spiritually as he or she is physically and mentally, then there are some practical steps you can take.*

**Parent/toddler groups.** Most churches have a parents and toddlers group. It's worth inquiring if your local church has one and taking your child along. You don't have to wait until she's "old enough"; it's never too soon to start, and even very small babies seem to enjoy watching other little children enjoying themselves singing and banging instruments!

**Thanksgiving and dedication.** You may want to think about dedicating your child (see 1 Samuel 1:27–28). Again, inquire at your local church. Usually there are some preparation sessions at which you will meet other couples and be able to find out together what the dedication service involves.

Many people would say that if you want the best for your child, that will certainly include praying that he will receive all God's gifts of forgiveness, love, and life, which are the great themes of these services, which will also provide a chance to give your baby a public welcome.

**Books of prayer and Bible stories**. We hope you will want to pray with your child, even from very early days. There are many lovely books of suitable prayers to get you started, most of them with large, bright pictures for Baby to enjoy. As well as the usual rhymes and stories, it can be a special treat at bedtime to read your child a story about Jesus or one of the great stories from the Old Testament. As he gets older, the books will become prized possessions.

**Praying for your child**. Above all, pray for your child (Philippians 4:6). When she is very, very tiny, pause by the cradle each night and put her into God's hands. Tell God what you want for her, and your worries and anxieties about her, too. To grow up "prayed for" is a great privilege for a child.

# Inspirational Library

Beautiful purse/pocket-size editions of Christian classics bound in flexible leatherette. These books make thoughtful gifts for everyone on your list, including yourself!

*When I'm on My Knees*      The highly popular collection of devotional thoughts on prayer, especially for women.
    Flexible Leatherette . . . . . . . . . . . . . . $4.97

*The Bible Promise Book*      Over 1,000 promises from God's Word arranged by topic. What does God promise about matters like: Anger, Illness, Jealousy, Love, Money, Old Age, and Mercy? Find out in this book!
    Flexible Leatherette . . . . . . . . . . . . . . $3.97

*Daily Wisdom for Women*      A daily devotional for women seeking biblical wisdom to apply to their lives. Scripture taken from the New American Standard Version of the Bible.
    Flexible Leatherette . . . . . . . . . . . . . . $4.97

*My Daily Prayer Journal*      Each page is dated and features a Scripture verse and ample room for you to record your thoughts, prayers, and praises. One page for each day of the year.
    Flexible Leatherette . . . . . . . . . . . . . . $4.97

Available wherever books are sold.
Or order from:

Barbour Publishing, Inc.
P.O. Box 719
Uhrichsville, OH 44683
http://www.barbourbooks.com

If you order by mail, add $2.00 to your order for shipping.
Prices are subject to change without notice.